CAPTURED
HISTORY

MIGRANT MOTHER

HOW A PHOTOGRAPH DEFINED THE GREAT DEPRESSION

by Don Nardo

Content Adviser: Kendall Miller, Adjunct Professor of
Journalism, Northern Michigan College

Reading Adviser: Alexa L. Sandmann, EdD, Professor of
Literacy, College and Graduate School of Education, Health,
and Human Services, Kent State University

COMPASS POINT BOOKS
a capstone imprint

Compass Point Books
151 Good Counsel Drive
P.O. Box 669
Mankato, MN 56002-0669

Editor: Jennifer Fretland VanVoorst
Designer: Tracy Davies
Media Researcher: Svetlana Zhurkin
Library Consultant: Kathleen Baxter
Production Specialist: Sarah Bennett

Image Credits

AP Photo/Jim McKnight, 35; Corbis/*San Francisco Chronicle*/Frederic Larson, 48;
DVIC/NARA, 58 (left); Franklin D. Roosevelt Library, 18, 57 (right); Getty Images/
Fotosearch, 7, 36; The Granger Collection, New York, 29, 33; Library of Congress,
cover, 5, 8, 9, 11, 13, 15, 16, 21, 22, 24, 25, 27, 37, 38, 39, 40, 42, 43, 45, 49, 51,
53, 55, 56, 57 (left), 58 (right); National Archives and Records Administration, 31;
Newscom/MCT/Ted Benson, 47, 59; NOAA/George E. Marsh Album, 20.

This book was manufactured with paper containing
at least 10 percent post-consumer waste.

Library of Congress Cataloging-in-Publication Data
Nardo, Don, 1947—
  Migrant mother : how a photograph defined the Great Depression / by Don Nardo.
    p. cm. — (Captured history)
  Includes bibliographical references and index.
  Summary: "Explores and analyzes the historical context and significance of the
iconic Dorothea Lange photograph"—Provided by publisher.
  ISBN 978-0-7565-4397-6 (library binding)
  ISBN 978-0-7565-4448-5 (paperback)
  1. United States—History—1933–1945—Juvenile literature. 2. United States—
History—1919–1933—Juvenile literature. 3. Depressions—1929—United States—
Juvenile literature. 4. Lange, Dorothea—Juvenile literature. I. Title.
  E806.N274 2011
  973.917—dc22
                              2010038578

Visit Compass Point Books on the Internet at *www.capstonepub.com*

Printed in the United States of America in North Mankato, Minnesota.
062011   006222R

TABLEOFCONTENTS

Chapter One

SNAPPING AN ICONIC PHOTO

A driving rain was falling on California's Highway 101 that March day in 1936. The driver, 40-year-old professional photographer Dorothea Lange, sat alone in the car. She later recalled what had been on her mind: "Sixty-five miles an hour for seven hours would get me home to my family that night, and my eyes were glued to the wet and gleaming highway that stretched out ahead."

Home for Lange was San Francisco, in northern California. She had just finished a monthlong picture-taking assignment in the southern part of the state. Working many days with little sleep had made her weary. So she could think of little else but her warm, dry house, her husband, and her young sons, Daniel and John. She had no inkling that in the next hour she would create a famous piece of history.

An Inner Argument

As she drove along the nearly deserted road, Lange suddenly saw something interesting. Later she described it as "a crude sign with pointing arrow which flashed by at the side of the road." In hand-written letters on the sign were the words "Pea-Pickers Camp."

She knew full well what those words meant. The U.S. economy was just beginning to recover from the Great Depression, a terrible worldwide economic downturn. But tens of millions of people in the United States were

Dorothea Lange was a photographer for the Farm Security Administration.

still out of work. Many jobless moved from place to place seeking temporary work picking fruit and vegetables— any opportunity to make a few dollars. The camp the sign mentioned, Lange realized, must be where local pea pickers had pitched their tents.

Lange passed the sign and had no intention of stopping. But then she was torn by what she later described as "an inner argument." Among the questions she asked herself were:

"Dorothea, how about that camp back there? What is the situation back there?

"Are you going back?

"Nobody could ask this of you, now could they?

"To turn back certainly is not necessary. Haven't you plenty of negatives already on this subject? Isn't this just one more of the same? Besides, if you take a camera out in this rain, you're just asking for trouble. Now be reasonable, etc., etc., etc."

Lange drove on for about 20 miles (32 kilometers). All the while she kept making excuses for why she had no good reason to visit the pea pickers' camp. Finally powerful curiosity overcame her excuses. She made a U-turn, drove back, and turned off the highway at the sign. At that point, she said later, "I was following instinct, not reason."

"As if Drawn by a Magnet"

By the time Lange reached a cluster of small tents and makeshift shelters, the rain had tapered off. Almost immediately, a possible subject for her camera lens caught

"I was following instinct, not reason."

Dorothea Lange's photographs of a migrant family in their makeshift shelter at a camp in California became her most famous and influential work.

her eye. A woman and four children sat beneath a crude tent with one side open to the elements. They seemed to be doing their best to avoid the soggy, muddy ground.

Lange parked her car and moved closer. "I saw and approached the hungry and desperate mother, as if drawn by a magnet," she later said. "I do not remember how I explained my presence or my camera to her but I do remember she asked me no questions." Lange took six photographs. Altogether the encounter lasted only about 10 minutes,

DO WE DARE LOOK AT OURSELVES?

Lange photographed Nettie Featherston, a migrant mother of three in Childress, Texas, in 1938.

Dorothea Lange strongly believed that the topic of poverty needs to be examined and re-examined regularly. In her view, human societies do not pay enough attention to poverty. That is one reason, she said, that it continues to be a problem. Through her photos, she hoped to do her part in solving that problem. Shortly before her death in 1965, she told an interviewer:

"The subject of poverty has to be unearthed and looked at again. ... Real poverty is when life doesn't meet the human needs, when the circumstances just simply don't yield it, and can't, no matter how the people struggle. ... What has produced the thing ... we call poverty? Not the plight of the people who endure it, but out of what it comes, and the many kinds of poverty that there are. ... No one has photographed, so far as I know, the social phenomenon of prosperity. It is unrecorded. No country has ever closely scrutinized itself visually that I know of. ... I know what we could make of it if people only thought we could dare look at ourselves."

she later estimated. As she worked, she asked the mother how old she was. The woman replied that she was 32. "She said that they had been living on frozen vegetables from the surrounding fields, and birds that the children killed," Lange later wrote. "There she sat in that lean-to tent with her children huddled around her."

Having snapped the photos, Lange decided to leave. "I did not approach the tents and shelters of other stranded pea-pickers," she remembered. "It was not necessary. I knew I had recorded the essence of my assignment." But although she knew the photos were good, she did not yet know just *how* good. Lange did not realize that one of the

Lange's photographs of a migrant mother and her family helped make Americans aware of the plight of migrant workers.

pictures would become iconic—perfectly capturing the spirit of the Great Depression. Photographer Michael Stones later described the timeless photo:

> *The iconic image is a close-up. Two of [the] children are behind [the mother] and back-on, leaving little doubt about who is the central figure. She looks away from the camera, her face thoughtful, worried, her body inclined toward the flimsy dwelling, a baby on her lap. Her right hand, placed prominently against the face, pulling down the corner of a lip, shows a delicacy of manner that contrasts with the dirt under its nails.*

These six heartrending images concisely and powerfully told a sad tale. They showed the plight of the mother and her children. But they also stood for something bigger. They captured the predicament that hundreds of thousands of migrant workers found themselves in. According to author and photographer Anne W. Spirn, "A photograph can embody a complete thought or an entire story. A series of photographs can shape a narrative or make an argument."

As she drove back toward Highway 101 that day, Lange may have realized that she had not asked for her subject's name. In fact, she would never find out. When Lange died three decades later, neither she nor the American public knew the identity of the woman who had come to be called the Migrant Mother.

Lange's iconic photograph came to symbolize the Great Depression.

Chapter Two

A NATION FALLEN ON HARD TIMES

The American people eventually learned the identity of the woman long known as the Migrant Mother. In the late 1970s, an article in a California newspaper revealed that it was Florence Owens Thompson.

The story of Thompson's life became public along with her name. It confirmed what many people had already guessed. The circumstances that brought Thompson and her family to the migrant workers' camp in March 1936 were the same ones that Dorothea Lange was working to document. The two women had never met before the day the photos were taken. But they were drawn together, along with many other Americans, because of a crisis that affected them all.

The Great Depression was a series of major economic setbacks affecting people of all walks of life. The setbacks created hard times and suffering for millions of people. To understand how Thompson and Lange came together when and where they did, one must look at the cause and massive scope of the Depression.

Financial Collapse and Job Losses

The Great Depression was set in motion by the collapse of the stock market. In late October 1929, the New York Stock Exchange experienced several huge financial losses. Investors lost $14 billion on October 28 and $15 billion the next day. Total losses for the month came to an incredible

People on the street gathered as policemen told of the stock market collapse and bank closures.

$50 billion, which would be equivalent to many hundreds of billions today. Moreover, in the months that followed, the market continued to bleed money.

The staggering losses produced a series of events that sent the entire U.S. economy into a downward spiral. In a sort of domino effect, one calamity triggered another, which caused still another. In the words of a modern expert:

[Many people] found themselves with much less [money] than they had thought they had, or with nothing at all. By [the] millions they quit buying anything except what they had to have to stay alive. This drop in spending threw the stores into trouble, and they quit ordering [new products] and discharged clerks. When orders stopped, the factories shut down, and factory workers had no jobs.

Job losses were the most obvious and crippling effect of the Depression. The U.S. unemployment rate rose to 9 percent by the start of 1930. It continued to go up until it reached an appalling 25 percent. That meant one of every four Americans wanting to work had no job.

Making matters even worse, tens of millions of Americans lost most or all of their life savings. This happened because many banks, like other businesses, suffered catastrophic losses. Between 1929 and 1933, more than 9,000 U.S. banks went under. As a result, the money people had deposited simply disappeared.

Living in Tents and Shacks

The collapsing markets, job losses, and bank failures combined to produce a marked and frightening increase in poverty. Many millions of Americans no longer had enough money to make ends meet. Some could no longer pay their mortgages or rent, so they became homeless. Entire families had to live in back alleys, in their cars,

"[Many people] found themselves with much less [money] than they had thought they had, or with nothing at all."

or in tents pitched in fields or the woods. Some found shelter in abandoned houses. Others lived in shacks they built with used lumber and other materials they found in garbage dumps.

A migrant workers' camp outside Marysville, California, was built of boxes, boards, and barrels—whatever material was available.

A traveler passing through Alabama in 1937 told about seeing such a makeshift hut. It housed six people—a father, mother, and four children. The shack had no electricity, running water, or toilets. According to the traveler:

> The cabin sits low to the ground, with a single layer of boards for a floor; one window, or rather window hole, in each room (no glass, a wooden shutter instead); a roof that leaks so badly that when the last baby was born, the mother said, her bed had to be moved three times; walls without paper or plaster, of course—indeed you can see daylight through their cracks.

Children of date pickers stood in the door of their makeshift home in Coachella Valley, California, in 1935.

Even worse was the situation of an Oklahoma family of nine. According to an observer, they lived in "a hole in the ground" into which they had stuffed a few chairs and other furniture items. "They had the dirt all braced up there," the person remembered, "just like a cave."

Some homeless families roamed from town to town or state to state. They searched for whatever temporary jobs they could find. These migrants also lived in tents or other flimsy shelters set up in back lots or fields. It was just such a migrant camp that Florence Thompson and her family were in when Dorothea Lange encountered them.

Waiting in Line for Bread

The residents of migrant camps, along with other homeless people, often lacked the money to buy food. So many of them suffered at times from starvation. In cities many of the poor lined up each day to receive small portions of bread distributed by charities. In New York City, a musician named Yip Harburg saw such breadlines nearly every day. He later wrote:

> Fellows with burlap on their shoes were lined up all along Columbus Circle, and went for blocks and blocks around the park, waiting [for hours to get a few morsels of food]. The prevailing greeting at that time, on every block you passed, by some poor guy coming up, was: "Can you spare a dime?" Or: "Can you spare something for a cup of coffee?"

"Can you spare something for a cup of coffee?"

People in New York City waited in long lines to receive free or discounted meals.

Moved by these cheerless scenes, Harburg wrote a song. "Brother, Can You Spare a Dime?" became widely popular because so many millions of Americans could identify with its sad but true-to-life lyrics. They say in part:

> They used to tell me I was building a dream,
> with peace and glory ahead.
> Why should I be standing in line just waiting
> for bread? ...
> Say, don't you remember, they called me Al?
> It was Al all the time.
> Say, don't you remember I'm your pal! Buddy,
> can you spare a dime?

The reality was that a great many Americans were so bad off that they could *not* spare a dime. A woman who worked for one of the charities that gave food to the homeless later described a family she knew that lived for 11 days on a few loaves of stale bread. She also recalled another destitute family. The mother "went along the docks and picked up vegetables that fell from the wagons. Sometimes the fish vendors gave her fish at the end of the day. On two different occasions, the family was without food for a day and a half."

Escape from the Dust Bowl

These were the harsh conditions in which Thompson and her family found themselves. Their personal plight stemmed in part from the fact that they were western farm workers. Farm workers were in dire straits all over the country. But life was particularly difficult for those who lived in the West.

Worst off were the residents of the so-called Dust Bowl. It covered large parts of Oklahoma, Texas, Colorado, New Mexico, and Kansas. During the 1930s the region suffered from a serious drought. The topsoil had become infertile from poor farming practices. In addition, it got so dry that a lot of it crumbled and blew away, sometimes feeding enormous dust storms. To escape the infertile soil and dust storms, more than half of the people in the area moved away.

A dust storm approached homes in Stratford, Texas, as people watched outside.

STEINBECK'S HOMELESS AND HUNGRY

Lange photographed a family of 11 preparing to sell their belongings for money to buy food.

The renowned American writer John Steinbeck was one of many Americans who was moved by Dorothea Lange's *Migrant Mother* photo. He later said that it had been one of the main inspirations for his novel *The Grapes of Wrath*. Now seen as a classic, the 1939 book explored the difficulties experienced by a family of migrants in the West. In this excerpt, thousands of desperate people head for what they hope will be a better life in California:

"Car-loads, caravans, homeless and hungry; twenty thousand and fifty thousand and a hundred thousand and two hundred thousand. They streamed over the mountains, hungry and restless—restless as ants, scurrying to find work to do—to lift, to push, to pull, to pick, to cut— anything, any burden to bear, for food. The kids are hungry. We got no place to live. Like ants scurrying for work, for food, and most of all for land."

Among those who fled were Florence Thompson and her family. In 1934 they left Oklahoma and headed west to California. They were not alone. The state soon became the most popular destination for homeless people in the West. According to scholar Mark Durden:

> *American farmers suddenly started flooding in with their families, driven from their farmsteads in the Great Plains states by a combination of*

Many farmhouses in the Dust Bowl stood unoccupied, abandoned as their former residents moved west.

the process of farm mechanization, the effects of the Depression and a series of droughts and dust storms that began late in 1933. Up until 1939, some 350,000 farmers deserted their homesteads and headed for California.

Growing Up Poor

For Thompson, going to California was in a way a kind of homecoming. The 1934 trip was the second time she had left Oklahoma for the West Coast. Her given name was Florence Leona Christie. A Cherokee Indian, she was born September 1, 1903, in Cherokee Nation, an Indian reservation in northeastern Oklahoma. She grew up near Tahlequah, the town where the tribal government was located. Like most others who lived on the reservation, she knew only poverty as a child.

In 1921, when she was 18, the young woman married Cleo Owens, then 23. In 1922 the couple moved to the California town of Shafter, about 18 miles (29 km) northwest of Bakersfield. Four years later they moved again, this time to a small town in northern California, where Cleo Owens had relatives. They did farm work and other low-paying jobs until 1931, when Cleo Owens died of tuberculosis. At the time Florence was pregnant with their sixth child.

During the next two years, Florence Owens kept working for local farmers. She was financially strapped, as she always had been. To supplement her income, she took a night job in a restaurant. In time she met and fell for a man from a well-to-do family, and they had a child together—her seventh. The relationship soon soured, however. She feared that the man's family might try to gain custody of the new baby. So in 1933 she and her children headed back to Oklahoma.

Less than a year passed before droughts and the onset of the Dust Bowl forced Owens to move again. With her children and parents, she returned to Shafter, in southern California. There she became involved with a man named James R. Hill and had another child. With the Depression at its lowest point, there was very little work to be had. To provide food for the family, the couple became migrant

In 1936 Lange noted that she passed 28 loaded cars on California's Highway 99 in only 45 minutes.

farmers, moving from one town to another. (Florence's eventual last name, Thompson, came from her last husband, George Thompson. They married in the 1940s, after the Depression had ended.)

A Desperate Lifestyle

Being migrant farm workers was hard on all members of the family. Florence Thompson's children attended school when they could. But mostly they toiled in the fields with their parents. One of the children, Katherine, later recalled that her mother put the youngest children in cotton sacks.

Lange photographed a young cotton picker with her empty sack at a migrant camp in Kern County, California, in 1936.

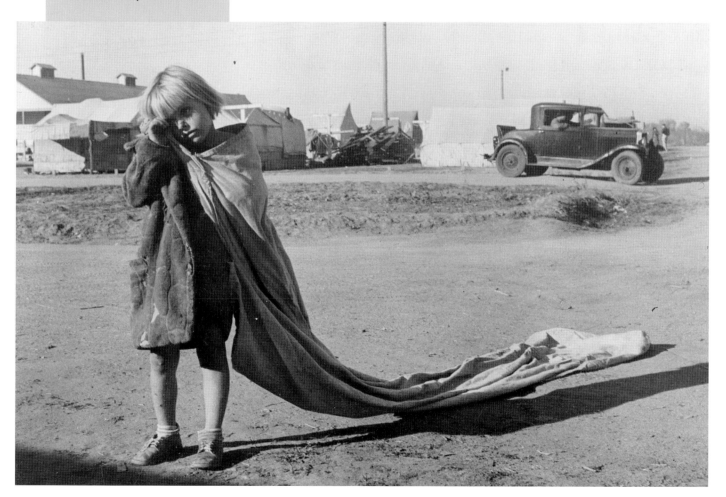

She carried or pulled the sacks as she picked vegetables or cotton. The older children walked ahead of her. "We would pick the cotton and pile it up in front of her," Katherine recalled. "And she'd come along and pick it up and put it in her sack."

Even when the children managed to make it to school, their lives were no easier. Because they lived in a car or tent, they rarely had a chance to bathe. So their classmates often teased them. "They'd tell you, 'Go home and take a bath,'" Katherine remembered. "You couldn't very well take a bath when you're out in a car [with] nowhere to go."

In March 1936 the family was still trapped in the difficult conditions. It was then that their fateful meeting with Dorothea Lange took place. Thompson, Hill, and the children finished picking beets in southern California, near the Mexico border. Then they drove northward on Highway 101, headed for Watsonville, on the central California coast. There they hoped to find more fieldwork.

The car broke down near the pea pickers' camp, which was near Nipomo. While trying to fix the vehicle, Hill accidentally damaged the radiator. So he and Thompson's sons removed the part, hitched a ride, and took it to the nearest town for repair. They left Thompson and the girls at the camp. It looked as if they would have to spend the night there. So the mother and her oldest daughters threw together a crude lean-to. The weary and worried mother was about to nurse her 1-year-old, Norma. Then she noticed a stranger approaching, a woman carrying a camera.

"You couldn't very well take a bath when you're out in a car [with] nowhere to go."

Two children of migrant fruit pickers stood at the door of their temporary home.

Documenting a Human Tragedy

The woman was, of course, Dorothea Lange. The long, winding route she had taken to the Nipomo camp was quite different from Thompson's. Lange was born May 26, 1895, in Hoboken, New Jersey. When Dorothea was 12, her father, Henry Nutzhorn, deserted her and her mother, Joan Lange. Left to be raised by her mother, Dorothea dropped the name Nutzhorn and took her mother's last name, Lange.

Dorothea Lange had a middle-class, fairly privileged upbringing. She got a good education. After high school she studied with the famous photographer Clarence H. White at his respected School of Modern Photography, in New York City. She then apprenticed with the renowned portrait photographer Arnold Genthe.

In 1918, when she was 23, Lange moved to San Francisco. She opened a portrait studio, which quickly became successful. Unlike many businesses, Lange's studio remained profitable during the Depression. She could have continued to make a comfortable living creating portraits for people able to afford that luxury. But she decided she wanted to photograph poor and homeless people. She later recalled what was for her a pivotal moment in 1933:

> There in my studio on Montgomery Street, I was surrounded by evidence of the Depression. ... I remember well standing at that ... window and just watching the flow of life. ... The unemployed would drift up there, would stop, and I could just see they

"The unemployed would drift up there, would stop, and I could just see they did not know where next."

Dorothea Lange wanted to use the camera to try to change the way the public saw the poor.

did not know where next. ... The studio room was one flight up, and I looked down as long as I could, and then one day said to myself, "I'd better make this happen."

What Lange meant by "this" was documenting the lives of the poverty-stricken masses. By showing their lives in photos, she hoped to call attention to the ongoing human tragedy. The next day she grabbed her camera, loaded it with film, and made her way into the crowded streets. There, that same day, she took what became her most famous photo aside from *Migrant Mother*. Titled *White Angel Breadline*, it captured the desperation of a hungry man standing in a breadline.

That and other photos Lange took of the human toll of the Depression soon caught the eye of government officials. Among them was Roy Emerson Stryker. He ran a federal program called the Photography Project, part of the Farm Security Administration. Stryker hired Lange and other gifted photographers to go out and document the suffering of the nation's poor.

Lange completed a photo shoot for Stryker in the Los Angeles area in March 1936. She was on her way back to San Francisco when she passed the pea pickers' camp near Nipomo. There she spent 10 minutes snapping six photos. One of them would come to immortalize both her and her subject, Florence Owens Thompson. In this way, two vastly different lives briefly came together and laid bare the soul of a suffering nation.

White Angel Breadline is one of Lange's first—and most famous—photos of the poor.

Chapter Three

TO CAPTURE THE CAREWORN

To this day, no one knows exactly what happened from moment to moment as Dorothea Lange photographed Florence Owens Thompson. It was, after all, a quick, spur-of-the-moment event. It also occurred long ago. But much of what happened can be reconstructed from the surviving evidence. Part of the evidence is the recollections of the participants—Lange, Thompson, and the children.

Even more important is the evidence of the photos themselves. In the years since they were taken, photographers and other experts have studied them closely. Various elements of these pictures are extremely informative. One element is the way in which Lange posed her subjects. It reveals much of what she was doing and saying in those fateful 10 minutes.

Photos Do Not Lie

In a magazine interview in 1960, Lange recalled what happened that day in 1936. She told about driving along Highway 101 and passing the pea pickers' camp. Eventually, she said, she turned around and drove back to the camp. One of the first things she saw in the camp was Thompson's lean-to. Of course, Lange did not know that the mother and her daughters had built the shelter less than an hour before.

Lange decided the lean-to and its residents would be excellent subjects. She had an extremely keen eye.

Lange spent much of her time on the road in search of photo opportunities.

Indeed, her ability to know which people and objects had something to say to the camera lens was uncanny. She would not have approached the mother and children if she had not seen their potential as subjects.

How Lange got Thompson to agree to be photographed is less certain. "I do not remember how I explained my presence or my camera to her," Lange said. "But I do remember she asked me no questions." Thompson's daughter Katherine McIntosh recalled a brief conversation between the two women. "She asked my mother if she could take her picture," McIntosh said in a 2008 interview. She said Lange had told Thompson that her "name would never be published, but it was to help the people in the plight that we were all in, the hard times. So mother let her take the picture, because she thought it would help."

In whatever manner Lange got Thompson and the girls to pose, the woman with the camera proceeded to take six photos. They start at a distance from the lean-to. Then, shot by shot, they move closer to the subjects. This technique was—and remains—common among portrait photographers, which Lange had been.

Another way the photos provide valuable evidence of the event and its subjects is through their captions. Lange and her colleagues in the Photography Project realized the importance of documenting the time, place, and other crucial details of their photos. Lange knew that without captions such information would likely be lost over time. So each of the six photos she took of Thompson bears a caption. One of

"I do not remember how I explained my presence or my camera to her. But I do remember she asked me no questions."

Migrant Mother **is the last and most famous of the six photos Lange took of Florence Owens Thompson and her children. The photographs are often displayed as a series.**

the shortest reads: "Destitute pea-pickers in California; a 32 year old mother of seven children." A longer one says:

> *Nipomo, Calif. Mar. 1936. Migrant agricultural worker's family. Seven hungry children. Mother aged 32, the father is a native Californian. Destitute in a pea-pickers camp, because of the failure of the early pea crop. These people had just sold their tent in order to buy food. Most of the 2,500 people in this camp were destitute.*

The Six Photos

The captions are helpful in recreating the famous scene. But they do not convey as much information as do the images themselves. The first of the six photos is a case in point. It was taken at a distance of about 30 feet (9 meters) from the lean-to. Unlike the other shots, it was not posed. This suggests to modern experts that Lange snapped it immediately after unpacking her camera. Her purpose may have been to give the viewer a feeling for the larger scene. It shows Thompson holding the baby, Norma, while Katherine stands beside her mother. Ruby, barely visible, hides behind Thompson, and teenager Viola sits in a small rocking chair facing her mother and sisters.

Thompson's two sons had gone into town with Jim Hill, so just she and four of her daughters were in the tent when Lange arrived.

The second picture is much more planned than the first. Also taken from a distance, it shows that Viola has moved the rocker outside the lean-to. Behind her, Thompson (still holding the baby), Ruby, and Katherine are lined up inside the tent. This time all are facing the camera. It is clear from the way they are arranged that Lange had hastily posed them.

Viola (in rocking chair) had spent most of her 14 years moving from place to place, making it difficult to receive an education.

The third photo in the shoot is a much closer shot. It only shows Thompson nursing Norma. Even today most people are unfamiliar with it. Photographer Michael Stones tells why:

There are many reasons why [this photo] failed to become famous. Most compelling is that the Migrant Mother *overwhelmed others in the series because of the power of its depiction of Florence's plight. Also, newspapers of the time were unlikely to print a picture of a woman breast-feeding. … [In addition, the picture] conveys a different message from the rest of the series. … [It] is less about Florence's plight than her fitness to nurture despite that plight. A message that life goes on despite [extreme poverty] was not at the top of an agenda that Stryker's agency sought to publicize.*

Thompson nursed 1-year-old Norma. Thompson would go on to have a total of 10 children.

The third photo is also memorable because of the different sort of symbolic message it sends. Lange knew the image of the mother holding and nursing her child would remind viewers of the Virgin Mary and baby Jesus. Indeed, for that reason *Migrant Mother* is sometimes referred to as *Migrant Madonna*.

The fourth and fifth photos in the series are slightly closer shots. And they are more carefully posed than the earlier ones. One shows Thompson holding the baby while Ruby rests her chin on her mother's left shoulder. Lange felt that it came close to capturing the plight of the homeless migrants. But she knew she could improve on it, which experts agree she did.

The determination on Thompson's face contrasts with 5-year-old Ruby's look of resignation.

In the other shot, Ruby's cheek rests on Thompson's shoulder, and the girl's expression is appropriately forlorn. Also, Lange made sure to move Thompson's well-worn locker trunk into the foreground. It reminds the viewer that migrants must be always on the move in order to eke out a living. An even more important detail is the empty pie tin resting on the trunk. Lange realized it would be a symbol of the widespread hunger the Depression had caused.

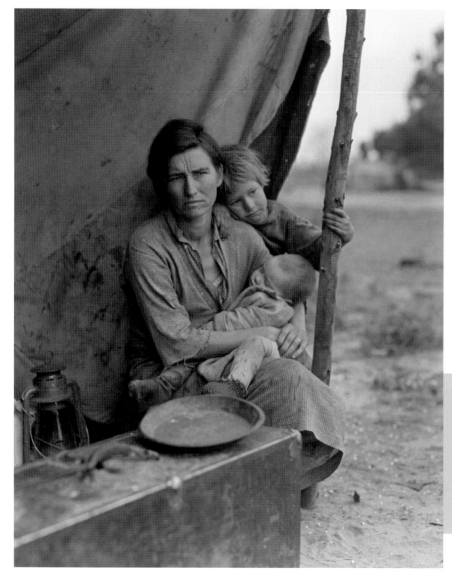

Thompson later complained that Lange's photographs simplified her circumstances and reduced her to a stereotype.

As moving as the fifth photo is, Lange once more topped herself. The sixth and last image in the series became the famous *Migrant Mother* photo. It was the only close-up of the six photographs.

A number of factors make the photo uniquely memorable and iconic. First, close-ups, by their nature, create feelings of intimacy. Second, the viewer shares those feelings with a woman who has a careworn face and an anxious expression. There is a strong impression that the mother's uneasy manner stems from worries about her children.

Adding to the bleakness of the scene is Lange's positioning of her subjects. Thompson is caught between her poverty-stricken children, evoking a feeling of entrapment. That Ruby and Katherine are hiding their faces suggests that they are ashamed of their situation. And the woman holds an infant dressed in soiled clothes. These images create a powerful feeling that Thompson is weighed down by the responsibility of caring for a large family in desperately hard times.

In this single photo, therefore, Lange was able to capture a wide range of emotions. They include fear, shame, and worry. Also obvious in the image is the haunting reality of the poverty and desperation of the Depression. It is no wonder that people everywhere immediately understood the photo's message. It was, as University of Delaware historian James Curtis so aptly says, "a pose that would burn itself into the memory of American culture."

"... a pose that would burn itself into the memory of American culture."

THE THUMB: MISTAKE OR HAPPY ACCIDENT?

The unretouched photo shows Thompson's left thumb.

Dorothea Lange concentrated extremely hard on getting her subjects into just the right pose for the sixth photo. She was so caught up in her work, in fact, that she failed to notice a small error. When Florence Thompson lifted her right hand to her face, as instructed, evidently she worried she might lose her balance. So she grasped the tent post with her other hand. Only after developing the film did Lange see the result. Thompson's thumb was visible in the picture's right foreground.

In the retouched photo Thompson's left thumb is absent.

The photographer felt that the thumb was a mistake that detracted from the beauty and impact of the photo. But her boss, Roy Stryker, disagreed. He thought the thumb was a happy accident that made the picture look more authentic. So he urged her to keep it in the shot. Soon afterward, however, she had an assistant retouch the photo, eliminating the thumb.

Chapter Four

A TRUTH AS OLD AS HUMANITY

After leaving the Nipomo pea pickers' camp, Dorothea Lange finished her homeward journey to San Francisco. Certain that she had just taken some potentially important photos, she quickly developed the film. Sure enough, at least three of the six shots appeared worthy of public view. She was sure her boss, Roy Stryker, would be pleased.

Her immediate concern, however, was the fact that Florence Thompson and the other migrants in the camp appeared to be starving. Lange felt that publishing some of the pictures right away would call attention to their suffering. That, she hoped, would spur some government agency to send food and other relief supplies to the camp. The tactic worked. Lange sent the photos to the *San Francisco News*. It printed two of them (not including the *Migrant Mother* image) a couple of days later. The story accompanying them was headlined: "Ragged, Hungry, Broke, Harvest Workers Live in Squalor." The following day, March 11, 1936, the paper ran the *Migrant Mother* image beside an article about government anti-Depression programs.

The stories and pictures swiftly made it into newspapers across the country. One result, as Lange had hoped, was a public demand that the government help the Nipomo pea pickers. That same month a federal agency delivered 20,000 pounds (9,100 kilograms) of food to the camp.

But Thompson and her family were not there to

benefit from the relief supplies. Having repaired their vehicle, they had already moved on to their next migrant workers' job. What happened to Thompson in the years that followed did not become known to the public until several decades later.

Florence Thompson's Story

In the late 1930s and early 1940s, Thomspon and her family continued to work as agricultural migrants. During those years she and James Hill had three more children together. But they eventually grew apart. After World War II, which ended in 1945, Florence married hospital administrator George Thompson. He could afford to support her and the children. So for the first time, they had a stable, moderately comfortable life.

Many years passed. For more than three decades no one but members of the family knew that Thompson was the Migrant Mother in Lange's world-famous photo. Then, in 1978, a reporter for a newspaper in Modesto, California, got a tip. Someone claimed that the woman in the photo was living in a mobile home in Modesto. The reporter drove to the mobile home. Immediately she recognized Thompson, then 74, as the Migrant Mother.

The two spoke at length. To her surprise, the reporter found that Thompson was displeased with how Lange had behaved after taking the photos. "I wish she hadn't taken my picture," Thompson said. "I can't get a penny out of it. She didn't ask my name. She said she wouldn't sell the pictures. She said she'd send me a copy. She never did."

What Thompson did not know was that in the 1930s Lange was working for the federal government. That meant that the pictures she took were in the public domain. For that reason, Lange never received any direct payments for the Migrant Mother photos. But the images did help to advance her photography career.

Thompson's health soon deteriorated. In 1983 she was hospitalized with cancer and heart problems. She died in September of that year and was buried next to her husband,

"She said she'd send me a copy. She never did."

Not surprisingly Thompson was most comfortable living in a mobile home. She said she needed to be able to move if bad times hit.

George, in Hughson, California. On her headstone, these words follow her name: "Migrant Mother—A Legend of the Strength of American Motherhood."

Thompson's daughter Katherine McIntosh summed up her family's feelings about the photo in a later interview:

"We were embarrassed by that picture. We didn't want people to know we were poor. But we are proud of the story behind the picture."

Dorothea Lange's Story

Just as few people knew what happened to Thompson after 1936, Thompson had no idea what had become of Dorothea Lange. After leaving Thompson and her daughters in the Nipomo camp, Lange continued her work

Katherine McIntosh and her siblings continued to travel with their mother in search of work until 1945, when Thompson's marriage brought some stability to their lives.

with the Farm Security Administration. Week after week, she captured the plight of poor, displaced Americans. In particular, she documented the hardships of impoverished migrant workers like Thompson.

The photos were distributed for free across the nation. They drew attention to the many Americans who were suffering from the ravages of the Depression. That helped to

Many of Lange's photographs depicted the difficult life and determined spirit of Dust Bowl farmers.

stir up a public demand for the government to help them.

Lange's images of the downtrodden came to be seen as iconic photos. Even more, several of them were considered artistic masterpieces. For that reason, in 1941 Lange received a prestigious Guggenheim Fellowship, an award for photographic excellence. Four years later she gained another honor. The great American photographer Ansel Adams invited her to teach photography at the California School of Fine Arts. This was only one of many important photographic endeavors that Lange continued to busy herself with. In 1952 she cofounded the high-quality photographic magazine *Aperture*.

Unfortunately for Lange, in the last years of her life she suffered from a series of serious illnesses. She died in October 1965 at age 70. Lange's accomplishments were so great that she continued to be honored after her death. In December 2008, for example, she was inducted into the California Hall of Fame.

"She Is Immortal"

Another honor that Lange achieved after her death was the continuing fame of, and widespread love for, many of her photos. Of these, *Migrant Mother* came to be seen as representing the height of the art of documentary photography. Of the millions of photos taken during the Great Depression, it was easily the most famous. Roy Stryker of the FSA called the photo the ultimate image of the Depression era and a piece of photographic art. Speaking of

Many of Dorothea Lange's Depression-era photos have come to be seen as iconic.

Thompson's image in the picture, he remarked: "She has all the suffering of mankind in her but all of the perseverance too. A restraint and a strange courage. You can see anything you want to in her. She is immortal."

This evaluation of the photo was borne out during the decades that followed the Depression. The picture was reproduced in virtually every book about that historical era. Quite often it appeared on the cover or first page. It also received several other honors. One of the most visible was its use on a postage stamp. In 1998 the U.S. Postal Service issued a 32-cent *Migrant Mother* stamp as part of its Celebrate the Century series.

In the same year in which the stamp appeared, the New York auction house Sotheby's offered a copy of the photo. It was accompanied by handwritten notes made by Lange herself. Also included was her signature. The picture sold for $244,500. Four years later Lange's own copy of the photo was auctioned at another well-known New York auction house, Christie's. A lover of photographic art paid $141,500 for it. Other photos from the Migrant Mother series sold for large amounts of money in the years that followed.

The Migrant Mother image also has been used in other social contexts. They include various forms of pop art and economic and political advertising. A prominent example occurred in 1996. That year those in charge of President Bill Clinton's re-election campaign made a film titled *A Place Called America*. It showed the pages of a family photo album flashing by. Among the pictures in the album was *Migrant*

"You can see anything you want to in her. She is immortal."

BEAUTY FOR ITS OWN SAKE

Lange hoped her photographs would help publicize—and thus relieve—the suffering of migrant workers.

Dorothea Lange believed that every piece of art, including every photograph, has some sort of consequence, whether good or bad. She always tried to ensure that her photos would produce positive outcomes. In a 1964 interview, she said:

"I believe that everything, every human action, has consequences. [And] if you can come close to the truth, there are consequences from the photograph. ... The good photograph is not the object. The consequences of the photograph are the object, and I'm not talking about social work. It can be ... something that is extraordinarily beautiful for its own sake. ... The consequence of its beauty is the transmission of it; so that no one would say, 'How did you do it? Where did you find it?' But they would say, '[How wonderful it is] that such things could be.'"

Mother. The following year, the A&E Network ran an ad for its show *California and the Dream Seekers.* It showed a blonde woman driving a 1950s convertible down a California street. Visible in the background were several photos of times past. One showed an old gold prospector and his mule. Another showed the *Migrant Mother.*

More of an economic statement featuring the *Migrant Mother* appeared in 2005. The cover of *The Nation* magazine advertised its feature story, titled "Down and Out in Discount America." Plainly visible was the famous photo, this time with Thompson's dress colorized blue. She was also wearing a Walmart jacket.

A Tribute to Their Durability

Some have argued that such uses of Lange's most memorable photo cheapen it. Others have countered that all great ideas and images eventually become part of our ever-evolving culture. This is partly because they are so recognizable. The fact that they are very familiar is a tribute to their quality and durability, rather than an insult to their original meaning. Thus, no matter how photos like Lange's are used later, their original meaning is never lost. Their inner truth, captured by the camera's lens, continues to reach out to and move viewers in generation after generation.

Migrant Mother is one of the most requested photographs in the
Library of Congress' collection.

Timeline

1895

Dorothea Lange is born in New Jersey.

1903

Florence Owens Thompson is born Florence Leona Christie in Oklahoma.

1918

Lange moves to San Francisco, California.

1934

Thompson moves from Oklahoma to California.

1936

Lange photographs Thompson and her daughters in a migrant workers' camp near Nipomo, California.

1929

The U.S. Stock Market crashes, setting in motion the Great Depression.

1933

More than 9,000 U.S. banks fail; Lange begins photographing the poor and homeless.

Writer John Steinbeck's *The Grapes of Wrath* is published; it captures the plight of migrant workers in the Depression era.

1939

1941

Lange is awarded a Guggenheim Fellowship.

Timeline

1945

World War II ends.

1952

Lange cofounds a new photography magazine, *Aperture*.

1960

Lange, in a magazine interview, recalls photographing Thompson.

1983

Thompson dies of cancer.

1998

The U.S. Postal service issues a stamp showing the famous photo; a copy of the photo is auctioned at Sotheby's in New York City for $244,500.

1965

Lange dies of cancer.

Thompson says in a newspaper article that she is the subject of the *Migrant Mother* photo.

1978

The Nation magazine puts the *Migrant Mother* photo on its cover.

2005

2008

Lange is inducted into the California Hall of Fame.

Glossary

breadline: group of hungry people standing in line to receive food handouts

downtrodden: oppressed, or people who have fallen on hard times

Dust Bowl: large section of the midwestern and western United States that suffered from catastrophic drought and dust storms during the 1930s

iconic: widely viewed as perfectly capturing the meaning or spirit of something or someone

impoverished: very poor

induct: to install or introduce someone into a group or organization, especially in a formal ceremony

Madonna: Virgin Mary, or any representation of her

migrants (or migrant workers): poor, often homeless, people who move from place to place to find temporary jobs

perseverance: continuing despite obstacles or difficulties

prestigious: important or impressive

public domain: legal term for objects, images, songs, and so forth that belong to the public and therefore can be reproduced for free

squalor: filth, or impoverished conditions

Additional Resources

Further Reading

Doak, Robin S. *Black Tuesday: Prelude to the Great Depression*. Minneapolis: Compass Point Books, 2008.

Landau, Elaine. *The Great Depression*. Danbury, Conn.: Children's Press, 2007.

Sandler, Martin W. *The Dust Bowl Through the Lens*. New York: Walker Books for Young Readers, 2009.

Internet Sites

Use FactHound to find Internet sites related to this book. All of the sites on FactHound have been researched by our staff.

Here's all you do:
Visit *www.facthound.com*
Type in this code: 9780756543976

Source Notes

Page 4, lines 4 and 17: "Migrant Mother, 1936." EyeWitness to History. 12 July 2010. www.eyewitnesstohistory.com/migrantmother.htm

Page 6, lines 7, 9, and 23: Ibid.

Page 7, line 4: Ibid.

Page 8, sidebar, line 9: Anne W. Spirn, ed. *Daring to Look: Dorothea Lange's Photographs and Reports from the Field*. Chicago: University of Chicago Press, 2009, p. 5.

Page 9, lines 2 and 7: Ibid.

Page 10, line 4: Michael Stones. "The Other Migrant Mother." 12 July 2010. www.openphotographyforums.com/art_MICHAEL_STONES_001.php

Page 10, line 18: *Daring to Look: Dorothea Lange's Photographs and Reports from the Field*, p. xi.

Page 14, line 1: Gerald W. Johnston. *Franklin D. Roosevelt: Portrait of a Great Man*. New York: William Morrow, 1967, pp. 119–120.

Page 16, line 5: Katharine D. Lumpkin and Dorothy W. Douglas. *Child Workers in America*. New York: Robert M. McBride, 1937, p. 4.

Page 17, lines 2 and 4: Studs Terkel. *Hard Times: An Oral History of the Great Depression*. New York: Random House, 2000, p. 45.

Page 17, line 19: Ibid., p. 20.

Page 19, line 5: "Brother, Can You Spare a Dime?" Words by E.Y. Harburg, music by Jay Gorney. Diane Ravitch, ed. *The American Reader: Words That Moved a Nation*. New York: HarperCollins, 1990, p. 270.

Page 19, line 18: William Dudley, ed. *The Great Depression: Opposing Viewpoints*. San Diego: Greenhaven Press, 1994, p. 36.

Page 21, sidebar, line 10: John Steinbeck. *The Grapes of Wrath*. New York: Viking Press, 1939, pp. 317–318.

Page 22, line 6: Mark Durden. *Dorothea Lange*. New York: Phaidon, 2006, p. v.

Page 26, lines 2 and 9: Thelma Gutierrez and Wayne Drash, "Girl from Iconic Great Depression Photo: 'We were ashamed.'" 12 July 2010. www.cnn.com/2008/LIVING/12/02/dustbowl.photo/index.html

Page 28, line 22: *Daring to Look: Dorothea Lange's Photographs and Reports from the Field*, p. 3.

Page 34, line 6: "Migrant Mother, 1936."

Page 34, line 10: "Girl from Iconic Great Depression Photo: 'We were ashamed.'"

Page 35, lines 1 and 3: Library of Congress. "Dorothea Lange's 'Migrant Mother' Photographs in the Farm Security Administration Collection: An Overview." 12 July 2010. www.loc.gov/rr/print/list/128_migm.html

Page 38, line 1: "The Other Migrant Mother."

Page 41, line 26: James Curtis. *Mind's Eye, Mind's Truth*. Philadelphia: Temple University Press, 1991, p. 65.

Page 46, line 16: Geoffrey Dunn. "Photographic License." 12 July 2010. http://archive.newtimesslo.com/archive/2003-09-11/archives/cov_stories_2002/cov_01172002.html

Page 48, line 1: Carolyn Jones. "Daughter of 'Migrant Mother' Proud of Story." *SFGate/San Francisco Chronicle*. 23 Aug. 2009. 12 July 2010. www.sfgate.com/cgi-bin/article.cgi?f=/c/a/2009/08/22/MN4H18MESA.DTL

Page 52, line 1: Robert Hariman and John L. Lucaites. *No Caption Needed: Iconic Photographs, Public Culture, and Liberal Democracy*. Chicago: University of Chicago Press, 2007, p. 55.

Page 53, sidebar, line 6: *Daring to Look: Dorothea Lange's Photographs and Reports from the Field*, p. 5.

Select Bibliography

Curtis, James. *Mind's Eye, Mind's Truth*. Philadelphia: Temple University Press, 1991.

"Depression Mother." *Famous Pictures Magazine*. 2009. 12 July 2010. www.famouspictures.org/mag/index.php?title=Depression_Mother

Durden, Mark. *Dorothea Lange*. New York: Phaidon, 2006.

Elliot, George P., and the Museum of Modern Art. *Dorothea Lange*. Garden City, N.Y.: Doubleday, 1968.

EyeWitness to History. "Migrant Mother, 1936." 12 July 2010. www.eyewitnesstohistory.com/migrantmother.htm

Ganzel, Bill. *Dust Bowl Descent*. Lincoln: University of Nebraska Press, 1984.

Goggans, Jan. *Dorothea Lange, Paul Taylor, and the Making of the New Deal Narrative*. Berkeley: University of California Press, 2010.

Gordon, Linda. *Dorothea Lange: A Life Beyond Limits*. New York: Norton, 2009.

Gutierrez, Thelma, and Wayne Drash. "Girl from Iconic Great Depression Photo: 'We were ashamed.'" 12 July 2010. www.cnn.com/2008/LIVING/12/02/dustbowl.photo/index.html

Hariman, Robert, and John L. Lucaites. *No Caption Needed: Iconic Photographs, Public Culture, and Liberal Democracy*. Chicago: University of Chicago Press, 2007.

Jones, Carolyn. "Daughter of 'Migrant Mother' Proud of Story." *SFGate/San Francisco Chronicle*. 23 Aug. 2009. 12 July 2010. www.sfgate.com/cgi-bin/article.cgi?f=/c/a/2009/08/22/MN4H18MESA.DTL

Lange, Dorothea. "The Assignment I'll Never Forget: Migrant Mother." *Popular Photography*. Feb. 1960.

Library of Congress. "Dorothea Lange's 'Migrant Mother' Photographs in the Farm Security Administration Collection: An Overview." 12 July 2010. www.loc.gov/rr/print/list/128_migm.html

Library of Congress. "Exploring Contexts: Migrant Mother." 12 July 2010. http://memory.loc.gov/ammem/awhhtml/awpnp6/migrant_mother.html

Maksel, Rebecca. "Migrant Madonna." *Smithsonian Magazine*. March 2002. 12 July 2010. www.smithsonianmag.com/arts-culture/Migrant_Madonna.html

McElvaine, Robert. *The Great Depression: America 1929–1941*. New York: Random House, 1993.

McElvaine, Robert. *Down and Out in the Great Depression: Letters from the Forgotten Man*. Chapel Hill: University of North Carolina Press, 2007.

"Ragged, Hungry, Broke, Harvest Workers Live in Squalor." *San Francisco News*. 10 March 1936.

Rubio, Oliva M., et al. *Dorothea Lange: The Crucial Years*. New York: La Fabrica, 2009.

Shlaes, Amity. *The Forgotten Man: A New History of the Great Depression*. New York: HarperCollins, 2007.

Spirn, Anne W., ed. *Daring to Look: Dorothea Lange's Photographs and Reports from the Field*. Chicago: University of Chicago Press, 2009.

Stones, Michael. "The Other Migrant Mother." 12 July 2010. www.openphotographyforums.com/art_MICHAEL_STONES_001.php

Terkel, Studs. *Hard Times: An Oral History of the Great Depression*. New York: Random House, 2000.

Index